Email
The Manual

Email
The Manual

Everything You Should Know About
Email Etiquette, Policies and Legal
Liability Before You Hit 'Send'

Jeffrey Steele

 **Marion Street Press**

Portland, Oregon

ISBN 1-933338-15-6
Printed in U.S.A.

Published by Marion Street Press
4207 S.E. Woodstock Blvd. # 168
Portland, Ore. 97206-6267
USA
http://www.marionstreetpress.com

Orders and desk copies: 800-888-4741

To Kathleen Furore, who introduced me to the
publisher of my first book

Contents

Acknowledgments

This slim volume of advice and enlightenment owes its very existence to a small, talented group of people who took the time to share their wit and wisdom on the topic of email.

The list includes a chief executive officer, a philanthropist, college professors, authors, attorneys, business owners and executives, consultants and even the president of the American Academy of Etiquette. All gave generously of their time and insight, some of them enduring multiple callbacks to ensure their words and thoughts were expressed correctly.

If interested in contacting any of the individuals who helped in this volume's preparation, please visit the source list at the end of the book, where you'll find phone numbers, email addresses and/or Web sites for all of them.

Preface

Email: A Powerful Tool

In the early 1990s, it would have been difficult to find anyone who used email. Today, it would appear equally challenging to identify folks who don't use it in some way in their day-to-day professional or private lives – or both.

Email has become a pervasive tool, and an

exceptionally powerful one, remarks Dov Seidman, CEO of Los Angeles-based LRN, which helps companies and their people deal with legal and ethical issues they face on the job.

"Everything happens in email," Seidman observed recently. "People lead in email, manage in email and demonstrate respect or non-respect in email. Email is like a microscope. It magnifies qualities about the sender: How they lead, how they manage, how they collaborate and how they communicate. It gives real insight into the sender. Email is more than what's in the email itself."

Depending on how an individual uses the medium, he adds, he or she can create efficient, productive working dynamics, or communicate misunderstanding, confusion and distrust. We all have that option each and every time we click "Send."

But perhaps because email is so ubiquitous, few of us really give much thought to how we present ourselves when we send cyber messages. That represents a sea change from yesteryear's approach to business communication, notes San Francisco-based public relations executive Don Ferguson. In the past, businesspeople took pains to make sure every missive sent out under a company's letterhead was letter perfect, with a slick presentation and flawless spelling and punctuation.

To do less, he says, was to invite the recipient to think poorly not just of the writer, but the company he represented. The advent of email, however, has rendered that philosophy as obsolete as carbon paper and rotary phones.

"What we've done is gone away from being thoughtful in the way we look and feel in communications," Ferguson observes. "[Email is] sloppy communication that doesn't worry about style, about nouns, verbs and objects.

"We need to get people back to thinking, 'This is business.' And that everything we put in email is not just our communications, it's our company's communications. You're not sending emails that are you, they are the company."

A Reflection On Us?

Maybe it's not really surprising that today's business email leaves a great deal to be desired. In a way, much of the email we send and receive is the perfect representation of the society that transformed email into a household word.

Should it come as a shock, for instance, that in

a land where cut-off jeans and a t-shirt are deemed appropriate attire for just about any occasion — up to and possibly including a visitation with the Pope — that a lot of email is unkempt and slovenly?

Should we be astonished that in a nation where the mid-finger salute serves as an easily tossed-off expression of road rage, too much email is tactless and rude?

And in a country late to grapple with its epidemic of obesity, should anyone be taken aback at the abundance of bloated emails?

We as a society can do better. Just as we can work harder to present ourselves attractively and professionally, observe basic rules of decorum and strive to become fitter and healthier, we can unlearn the habits that have helped make too much email inappropriate for the professional business environments in which it is sent.

Aim Higher

As Ferguson says, email needs to be more "thoughtful." And maybe the way to achieve that goal is to keep the positive end results in mind as we craft our messages.

"The reason to write an email is to do something productive, to transmit and share information, or to collaborate and create a productive work experience with someone – and to do that with people in far-flung corners of the world," Seidman says. "Email allows you to have collaborations with people you wouldn't normally be able to collaborate with. So the question is: Do you want to be effective in that or not?"

If your answer is yes, you'll find the tools you need in the pages that follow.

Chapter 1

Civility in Cyberspace

Ford Motor Company philanthropist, etiquette expert and author Charlotte Ford has a very simple definition of etiquette. "It's showing consideration for other people," says Ford, the author of 21st Century Etiquette (Penguin, 2003). "It's not about knowing what shrimp fork to pick up. Just bear in mind how your actions affect others, and you're on the right track."

What works in the more traditional world of etiquette is just as essential, if not more so, in the realm of cyberspace. Considering how your email will impact recipients — including those to whom the email might be forwarded — is perhaps the biggest step in avoiding disaster.

So make that your number one priority. Before sending that email, think about the recipient's feelings. Consider his time commitments. Reflect on her ability to understand what you're writing and be able to act on it in an expeditious manner.

Old Meets New

Often, email and etiquette don't blend together comfortably, says Wendy Hart Beckman, Cincinnati-based author of *Communication Tools Made Easy* (Kendall/Hunt, 2004), who has taught classes in business writing. That's because while the most prolific users of email tend to be younger people, they are the very folks least likely to be schooled in the niceties of etiquette.

"I tell my business writing students they should take email as seriously as a memo to a co-worker or supervisor, or a business letter to a

17

client," she says. "I see young people sending very informal emails, palling with the recipient, when they're really not in that kind of relationship. Email has an implied informality, but it's not a true informality, especially in a business setting."

Cheryl Dellasega, professor of humanities at Penn State College of Medicine in Hershey, Pa., and author of *Mean Girls Grown Up* (Wiley, 2005), which features an appendix titled "Netiquette," knows the problem all too well.

"I teach medical students, and sometimes get emails from students who greet me, 'Hey Doc!,'" she says. "Or someone will say, 'Hi Cheryl,' using my first name. Follow rules of proper correspondence and use the recipient's title, especially on first contact.

"If I get a greeting like 'Hey Doc!' I'm likely to think, 'What's wrong with this person?' and take them less seriously. If you see that someone has taken the time to compose something using the correct title, and it's clear they've spent more than 30 seconds on the email, it makes a very positive impression, before you've even met them . . . Overly familiar emailing can color the recipient's perception of you."

Speed is part of the problem. Years ago, the writer of a business letter had plenty of time to think about what was being said, and perhaps change a few things. He could smooth over the syntax, ponder and perhaps soften the tone and consider how the recipient would respond.

Today, words are tossed quickly into the text field, the "Send" button is punched and only after it's gone do we think, "Maybe I shouldn't have called the vice-president by her first name."

Don't Forget Your Etiquette

With Charlotte Ford's lesson in mind, here are a few steps that will help you demonstrate appropriate levels of courtesy when sending business email:

Think about your subject line. Most people are inundated with email. Treat them with courtesy by crafting a subject line for your email message that briefly describes the message, helping them understand whether this is top priority, or can wait a bit, Beckman advises.

"A lot of people don't open their emails. They just skim the subject lines to determine whether

it's worth their time to open it, or whether they want to send it on to someone else," she says. "You want to give your reader some idea of what they need to do about that email."

Say you're the person in charge of organizing the company picnic this coming Sunday, and on Friday something happens that will necessitate its cancellation. A poor choice of subject lines to announce the cancellation would be "Company Picnic," Beckman says. A better line might read "Company Picnic Canceled." Best would be "Company Picnic Postponed Until (date)."

In keeping with Ford's advice, you're being sensitive enough to your recipients' feelings and priorities to recognize they'll want to know immediately of the cancellation, and will also want to learn that it hasn't been deep-sixed entirely.

To cite another example, you might need to send a negative email to your boss regarding a problem with a shipper, Beckman says. Don't simply dump the problem in the subject line. If possible, add the solution as well. "Shipper ABC on strike, Shipper XYZ on board."

Use a salutation and a signoff. You've gotten them by the boatloads: Emails that sail right ahead without a salutation. While acceptable in a correspondence with a friend or close relative you email regularly, the sans-salutation approach makes you look much too informal in the business setting, and may give your recipient the sense you're really too busy to show some respect, Ford says. "I think it should be as professional as a business letter," she observes.

By the same token, take a couple split seconds to say "thanks," "best regards" or some other closing, and offer your name. She may not perceive it consciously, but your recipient won't wind up feeling she isn't worth a couple extra seconds of your time.

Keep it brief. Flabby writing isn't just bad writing. In email, it's discourteous writing.

So be aware that the person to whom you're writing doesn't have all morning to wade through a bloated email. "We all have information overload," says Randy Hines, author with Joe Basso of *The Writer's Toolbox: A Comprehensive Guide for PR and Business Communication* (Kendall/Hunt, 2005).

"Be concise with your words," he says. "Be as

detailed as you can in as few words as possible. And if possible, keep your message all on one screen, which is about 25 lines or less. That forces you to be concise." An added benefit is that more of your emails will likely to be read, because they'll be more inviting to the eye of the beholders, Hines observes.

Get an Okay. If forwarding a message, get the okay of the individual who sent it, urges Philadelphia-based Lisa Taylor Richey, president of The American Academy of Etiquette.

"If there's something sensitive or confidential about that message, don't forward it unless you have the sender's permission," she says. "It may be a message they don't want released."

Know When Not to Email

Showing courtesy and appropriate email etiquette also means — in certain situations — getting out a pen and stamp rather than racing to the keyboard.

Such occasions would almost certainly include recognizing a gift giver's generosity, or extending an invitation to a wedding, dinner or cocktail party, Ford says.

Civility in Cyberspace

Early 20th Century writer Will Cuppy once quipped that etiquette means "behaving yourself a little better than you absolutely have to." Make it your principle in email, too.

| Send | Contacts | Spell | Attach | Security | Save | |

From: ED AVIS <edavis@marionstreetpress.com>   – edavis@marionstreetpress.com

To: Glenjones@umc.edu

To:

Subject: internship

Hi Doc! Your class has been a blast – especially the easy tests!

Can you find me an internship at the hospital this summer? I'd love to hang there with you!

Ed

Hmm, will Ed get this internship? Note the informal tone and overfamiliar attitude.

○ ○ ○   Compose: Internship at hospital this summer?

Send	Contacts	Spell	Attach	Security	Save	

From: ED AVIS <edavis@marionstreetpress.com>   – edavis@marionstreetpress.com

To: Glenjones@umc.edu

To:

Subject: Internship at hospital this summer?

Dear Professor Jones:

I've enjoyed your class this semester. I especially appreciated your fair tests.

Can you help me find an internship at the hospital this summer? I would truly enjoy the opportunity to work beside you there.

Sincerely,

Ed Avis

Okay, this is more like it.

Chapter 2

Keep it Professional

Hand in hand with etiquette goes professional-ism. It takes a rare blend of talent and charm to behave unprofessionally in work settings and still succeed. Most of us realize we must display some level of professional decorum to forge ahead. What starts as a chore in early stages of our careers becomes reflexive, natural and enjoyable as we advance. By that point, we've realized professionalism is a differentiating quality that can help us stand out from the pack.

Sadly, not all emailers in the world of business have absorbed that message. The American Academy of Etiquette's Lisa Richey says she's surprised by how many high-ranking corporate executives churn out emails loaded with lower-case i's and u's for *you*. Casual observers might assume they were penned by high school sophomores, not vice-presidents.

"Treat email like a business letter," she says. "Use correct punctuation and spellings. And always reread, even if you use spell check, because some incorrectly spelled words slip through."

Have you ever typed *you* when you meant *your*? Spell check will miss it every time.

Present Yourself Professionally

Pinkie Pushups. We realize that the wearisome shift key can often be an annoying consumer of time and effort in this fast-paced world. Nonetheless, avoid the temptation to write everything in capital letters or in lower case. "That

seems to be common among many students today," comments Susquehanna University's Randy Hines. "It seems to be quicker to not hit the shift key, but it seems to me the pinkies need to be exercised — especially in the business setting."

Consider what happens when you lock your email into all lower or upper case mode. With all lower-case letters, you give email recipients the impression you think you're poet e.e. cummings, or that they just aren't important enough for you to tap the shift key a few times. Remain in upper case, and it appears you're constantly SHOUTING, AND QUITE POSSIBLY ANGRY!

Salute to Salutations. You wouldn't start a business letter with "hi" or "hey," Richey says. So if you're sending off an email to a client or prospective client, a customer or a sales prospect or anyone who in an earlier day and age would have received a business letter, make sure it's addressed "Dear Mr. Smith," or "Dear Ms. Jones."

Says Richey: "When in doubt, refer to the person you're addressing formally."

Copying Blind. If you use distribution lists,

Richey recommends always using the blind carbon copy. This approach, which is most appropriate when sending an email to an extensive distribution list, will hide all email addresses to which you're sending the message.

Employing the blind carbon copy, abbreviated bcc, offers several advantages. First, it makes for a more professional-looking email, resulting in a missive that doesn't force recipients to scroll through dozens, scores or hundreds of names and email addresses to read. Second, it offers individuals on the list the sense their email addresses aren't being given out to everyone else on the list. The third benefit profits the sender. You may have worked very long and diligently to accumulate those contacts, Richey says. By using bcc, you're ensuring you're not passing those hard-earned names and addresses on to just anyone on the list.

Don't Try, Try Again. If you haven't heard back from someone days after sending him an email, do you send it again?

If it's imperative the recipient has received the message, you might consider emailing again and politely inquiring as to whether the original email

was received, Richey says. If there's still no response, pick up the phone and call him, rather than emailing a third time.

"On the flip side, I encourage people to use the out-of-office reply feature, to let people know you're not able to respond right away," she adds. Simply alerting email senders that you've received their email can be an act of professionalism and courtesy, she notes.

Just Say No. We've all received them cybernetically: Off-color jokes, chain letters, tasteless photos and illustrations and religious or political humor. There's no better way to unintentionally alienate people important to your career than by forwarding them an offensive email.

"They can be very distasteful," Richey says. "It's especially important to avoid them if you're emailing within a corporation . . . If it's a good idea to avoid off-color, political or religious humor or observations at a party, it's equally sound advice to avoid them in email."

Email Body Language :-)

There's a problem with email that we don't experience when speaking to someone in person

or over the phone, says author Wendy Hart
Beckman. Simply put, there's no way to convey
tone of voice or facial or body language in an
email. The problem? Those non-verbal cues often
are just as key to conveying messages as the
words chosen to communicate them.

"You can't tell the tone of voice in business letters either. But there, people tend to be flat and
very conservative in what they write," Beckman
observes. "In emails, by contrast, senders are
fooled by the implied informality. They might say
something sarcastic or tongue in check, and wind
up surprised when their reader is offended by it."

The situation may be more acute for women,
suggests author Cheryl Dellasega.

"Women more than men rely on facial expres-
sions, so they pick up on a lot of non-verbal cues,
as opposed to men, who focus on content," she
says. "If you don't think about how you write the
email, you can inadvertently miscommunicate . . .
You might write, 'This needs to be completed
quickly,' and intend only for that message to
encourage expeditious completion of the job. But
without the body language and other non-verbal
cues, the person on the receiving end might ask,
'Does this mean she thinks I usually don't com-

plete jobs quickly?'"

In an effort to solve the cybernetic problem of non-existent non-verbal cues, emailers soon found means of conveying amusement, light-heartedness or faux anger. They include emoticons (the yellow smiling, frowning and winking faces many email programs make available), the smiley created from colon-hyphen-close paren, and the ubiquitous laugh-out loud (LOL). All are about as appropriate in the office setting as an appearance in your robe and bedroom slippers.

In Beckman's eyes, they have no place in business documents because they're simply "too cutesy," she says. "They might give a clue as to your tone of voice, but might also clue your reader into the fact you tend not to make good business choices," she reports.

To keep it professional, avoid frivolous emoticons and other symbols of emotion at all costs, Beckman urges. Instead, give extra attention to your word choices. If it's crucially important the message not be misconstrued, write it in a word-processing program, print it out and have a second set of eyes look it over before you send it to the recipient, she says.

The bottom line? Injecting a time-honored

touch of professionalism into every business email won't make a career. But it certainly could prevent breaking one.

Send   Contacts   Spell   Attach   Security   Save

From: ED AVIS <edavis@marionstreetpress.com>   edavis@marionstreetpress.com

To: Franksmith@printers.com

Subject: our bid for your project

hi frank - did u get our price for printing that new cookbook...hope
smith didn't beat us 2 it.

hey, what were senator G's three hardest years? second grade! LOL

ed

Are you ee cummings? Then don't do the all-lowercase thing. And is it too much to ask to spell out "you"? Finally, save the political humor for another time.

Keep it Professional

Compose: Follow up on cookbook project

Send · Contacts · Spell · Attach · Security · Save

From: ED AVIS <edavis@marionstreetpress.com> ~ edavis@marionstreetpress.com

To: Franksmith@printers.com

Subject: Follow up on cookbook project

Dear Frank: I wanted to confirm that you received our bid for your cookbook project. I hope that we turn out to be the low bidder.

Please let me know if you need any other information.

Let's get together for lunch soon. I've got some new jokes to share with you.

Sincerely,

Ed Avis

This is professional and to the point.

Chapter 3

Getting and Keeping an Audience

Not everyone reads all of his or her email. For those who receive 100 or more emails a day, reading every word would be a full-time job in itself.

"Most people don't read email. They scan it,"

reports Ted Demopoulos, a Durham, NH-based consultant and writer on proper email technique.

"There are two reasons for that. A lot of us get far too much email. And even those who can manage their incoming email often try to answer email while doing something else."

Of course, you wouldn't take the time to write and send your missive if you didn't want your recipient to absorb the message. There's no guarantee he or she will, of course. But there are a few ways to improve the odds that yours will get opened — and read.

Tricks of the Direct Mail Trade

Direct mail writers know their recipients receive many commercial appeals every day. They also know they have to overcome two obstacles to bust through that clutter. First, they have to convince, tease or trick the recipient into opening the mailing. Then they have to get him or her to read what's inside.

You can use some of the same techniques that work for the most successful direct mail copywriters. Among the most important are the following:

Consider what your reader wants or needs to hear in the subject line. A line like "Good News on Assignment's Progress" or "Action Needed by 3 p.m." is more likely to result in an email being opened than a line like "Status Report" or "Update." It's the equivalent of the tease on an outside of a direct mail envelope, which if effective gets recipients to open the mailing.

Keep your writing style simple and direct. If sentences grow involved and convoluted, split them up. And use short words that are likely to be easily digestible if the recipient is skimming or quickly reading the email.

Use subheads. If you have a number of points to make and they begin to get complex, think about using short two- or three-word subheads at the beginning of each brief paragraph to summarize the sentences that follow.

Employ the short and punchy paragraph. Sometimes, a one-line paragraph is the single best way to get a very important point across.

Vary the length. Staggering the length of both sentences and paragraphs is a great way to keep the reader reading. A long stream of sentences and/or paragraphs of approximately the same length makes for a dull and monotonous email.

Inject some air into your message by providing plenty of white space. "You want to apply the principle known as 'chunking,'" author Wendy Hart Beckman reports. "Break it into pieces." The addition of a clean line between paragraph breaks provides needed white space and prevents readers from being repelled by a gigantic block of characters.

How often do you receive emails that serve up a single, monolithic block of copy? Not a line of white space. Not an underlined, italicized or highlighted word. Not a bullet. Not even a paragraph break from one thought to the next.

And how tempted are you to wade into that jungle?

Make one point per email. While Beckman urges emailers to keep each paragraph to one point, Demopolous takes it a step farther. "There should be only one important point per email," he

says. "If you have more than one point, they may not necessarily get to your second one."

Get to the point quickly. Readers will absorb your message more readily if you avoid dragging your feet in your opening lines. Get to the point in the first sentence.

Address resistance early. If your message is intended to be persuasive and you anticipate resistance, consider addressing those reservations right up front, Beckman says. If, for instance, you're seeking funds for a charitable cause, but know the person or group probably can't afford to contribute, you might acknowledge the likely inability to donate, but add there is still an opportunity to help by donating the time and efforts of volunteers.

Provide emphasis where needed. Most email systems allow you to do that several ways: through underlining, adding bold text, italics or even colored or highlighted text. Beckman prefers the use of underlining when she wants to call particular attention to a point in her email.

Don't use too many emphases. Emphasis is fine to break up copy and underscore key points, but shouldn't be done to death. Using underlining, bold and italics too much overwhelms the message and makes it appear you don't trust your readers to grasp the most important points.

Use bullets where appropriate. "I love bullets," Beckman says of the bold black dots you see leading key points. "They add white space and call attention to themselves. But bullets imply that order doesn't matter. Use numbers instead if there is some priority or sequence required. For instance, if issuing instructions to a subordinate, you might list the required duties you want done in the order they should be performed."

Send	Contacts	Spell	Attach	Security	Save

From: ED AVIS <edavis@marionstreetpress.com> – edavis@marionstreetpress.com

To: joesmith@hockey.com

Subject: sales proposal

Dear Joe: I'd like to introduce you to our new line of printing papers. I'm sure you'll find their bright white color suitable to all your printing needs. The color comes from our unique bleaching process, which is environmentally friendly but still creates an unsurpassed white color. The papers also hold ink remarkably well, and don't smear at all. We've got a good deal running on this product right now: buy three cartons and get the fourth free. Can I count on you for a big order? Thanks.

Ed

Which email is more likely to be read by the potential customer?

Getting and Keeping an Audience

```
○ ○ ○                    Compose: sales proposal                        ⊂⊃
 🖼          📇          ABÇ.        📎 .      🔒 .        📥.              ☀
Send       Contacts      Spell      Attach    Security     Save

From:  ED AVIS <edavis@marionstreetpress.com>  – edavis@marionstreetpress.com    ⊕

  ▾        To:  👤 joesmith@hockey.com



Subject:  sales proposal
```

```
Dear Joe:

I'd like to introduce you to our new line of printing papers. The
features include:

-Bright white color suitable to all your printing needs

-A unique bleaching process, which is environmentally friendly but still
creates an unsurpassed white color.

-Remarkable ink retention, without smearing

-A great price: buy three cartons and get one free.

Would you like to place an order? I look forward to hearing from you.

Sincerely,

Ed
```

Chapter 4

Big Brother is Watching

Author Wendy Hart Beckman recalls working at an engineering firm in the early days of email. One of the company's rising young stars, a gent envious co-workers referred to as the "Golden Boy," seemingly could do no wrong. He was clearly on a fast track to a corner office, if not the CEO's suite. Then one day, the Golden Boy's Midas touch turned to fool's gold.

He decided to send a blonde joke through the company's email system, assuming only he and his recipient would be in on the laugh. The following morning he was called into the office of his boss, who bestowed upon him not a promotion but a pink slip. "The company was backing up the network every night," Beckman says. "And they were also doing random email checks."

What turned into a painful lesson for the Golden Boy may help the rest of us avoid similar heartache. The message: Email should never be considered private. If you are emailing on your employer's network or system, the boss owns your email. And can read it.

The Emailing Mindset

Sadly, email's very informality tends to cloud our minds, leading us to assume what we're writing is only for the eyes of sender and recipient. That notion has been the undoing of many an employee who thought it okay to send questionable emails on company time, says lawyer Jeremy Mishkin. The Philadelphia-based attorney headed the American Bar Association's task force on

issues in cyberspace law. He also created a bibliography of cyberspace law that's been recognized as an industry standard by attorneys and lay people throughout the land.

According to Mishkin, an emailer's mindset comes closest to that of someone engaging in a private conversation with another individual in a closed room. Email feels like a private conversation, with no one but the participants hearing, he says.

In fact, he says, office email can be, and often is, monitored by employers.

"Whatever you're doing on the computer, whether it's email or Web browsing, is subject to company oversight," he says. "Some companies actually do randomly look into email on their system. Others use software that allows them to see how people are using the office computers on their desks, whether it's to do online shopping or download pornography."

Eric M. Rosenberg takes it one step further. "There are now vendors that offer systems for surveilling email, and some companies are engaging in that practice," says Rosenberg, a former Merrill Lynch senior litigator, and currently president of LitigationProofing, LLC, a Mamaroneck, NY firm that consults with organizations on email and electronic document retention, and trains employees at all levels in the do's and don'ts of business email.

"If you write a personal email on a company system where there is surveillance, it's likely to come to the company's attention if it includes inappropriate language or attachments, or references to inappropriate Internet addresses. It may come to the company's attention even if it involves totally appropriate matters, if a word being searched by the surveillance system pops up."

Corporate Email Policies

To set employees straight on the non-private nature of their emails, Mishkin recommends companies institute corporate email policies (see sample on page 86).

The first task, he says, is to raise employees' awareness. "They need to realize that pressing the 'Send' button is the same thing as signing a memo," he observes. "Once they do, they have a much greater respect for the medium, and there's a much diminished likelihood they will transmit a message they shouldn't."

Often, employers instituting such policies hire Mishkin to come in and present a 15-minute talk, explaining these realities to their workers. He enlivens his talk with real-world examples of emailers who have been stung.

For instance, he often relates the tale of a prominent New York City investment banker who wound up in hot water with federal investigators as a result of emails he sent his brokers. A number of his emails included his observation, "I wouldn't buy this stock, but go ahead and sell it to the dopey customers." Those emails often referred to such stocks with the acronym "POS" — and everyone on the receiving end knew that meant "piece of sh--."

"People witnessing this presentation recognize this message, and it strikes home with them," Mishkin reports. "It's the kind of message they've either received or sent."

The next task of employers instituting corporate email policies is to make clear to every user the computer system they employ at the office is governed by office policy, and is subject to inspection and review by the company. Once it's well known the company has the technology to monitor email and Web usage, employees tend to develop "a healthy self-awareness" that they wouldn't want to write something in email they wouldn't be proud to show their boss.

"These two steps eliminate an enormous percentage of the problem," Mishkin says.

Not Just Your Boss Watching

After coming to grips with the full extent of their employers' watchdog abilities, most folks aren't likely to send off malicious emails on company time. But they should also know that if they're inclined toward cybernetic nastiness even outside the office, they will find it increasingly difficult to remain incognito in a world where emails can be effectively and precisely traced.

"People sometimes think they can send email anonymously," Mishkin observes. "They will hide behind pseudonyms, pen names and aliases to allow them to say things they shouldn't say, and try to stir up trouble. They believe themselves to be immune from detection. And in some cases, I will be hired to go find them and stop them. And I've done that."

Mishkin reports it's increasingly common for companies targeted by electronic messages sent using false names to go to extra lengths to track

down the individual sending the messages. This kind of sleuthing meets with success far more often than many suspect.

One of Mishkin's most satisfying experiences came shortly after being hired by a client receiving email that was as venomous as it was anonymous. He tracked down the sender, got his phone number, called him and identified himself as the attorney for the company being targeted.

"I said to him, 'You are Mr. X. And I'm calling to let you know we know you are Mr. X, and to make sure that Mr. X never bothers the company again.'" Mishkin recalls.

On the other end of the line, there was a brief pause. And then Mr. X managed to stammer, "I don't know how you found me, but you'll never hear from me again."

"For a lawyer," Mishkin observes, "that was a Perry Mason moment."

Whether it's Perry Mason, Big Brother or your own boss you fear, stay clear of trouble. Never punch that "Send" button without assuming someone's reading over your shoulder.

Big Brother is Watching

```
000                        Compose: did you hear?

Send      Contacts      Spell      Attach   Security     Save

From:  ED AVIS <edavis@marionstreetpress.com>   - edavis@marionstreetpress.com

       To:  joesteffen@company.com

Subject:  did you hear?

Hey Joe - keep this to yourself, but I've got an interview with ABC Co.
next week. I'd love to blow this popsicle stand and tell you-know-how to
take a hike!

Ed
```

**Do you think you-know-who won't see this?
Think again.**

Chapter 5

Think Before You Email

Think about this. How many sleepless nights, demotions, firings, ulcers and quite possibly nervous breakdowns have resulted from pushing the "Send" button on an email too soon? The answer is certainly incalculable. But suffice it to say a whole lot of folks have experienced a world of angst over their failure to simply take a moment or two to think before sending an email they came to instantly or eventually regret.

Author Wendy Hart Beckman calls it the "Oh No Moment" – the instant you wish you could reach through your monitor's screen and reel in an ill-conceived email.

But it's too late.

Years ago, Beckman was on the receiving end of such a cybernetic posting. Her position called for her to gather data from departments within the company for which she then worked. Each month, she had to remind employees to provide the data, and some began kidding her about being a nag. "One month, a woman in the company meant to forward my reminder to someone else," she recalls. "But in the process, she added some nasty comments about me, such as who did I, the Queen Bee, think I was? Then she inadvertently hit 'Reply' instead of 'Forward.'"

Beckman read the email, saw red, and had to fight the urge to reply with a missive equally nasty. "I closed the email and walked away, and got a drink of water. I thought about how she must have felt when the message on her computer said she had sent it to me rather than the other co-

worker. I thought she must have felt terrible. And I enjoyed that," she remembers with a laugh.

"I replied to the woman, 'Dear Kathy: Thank you so much for your constructive criticism. I always appreciate feedback on my performance. And by the way, you might want to learn the difference between "Reply" and "Forward."' That may sound petty, but it was tame compared to what she called me."

Take Your Hands Off the Keyboard and Step Away From the Email

Significantly, by taking a break and giving some thought to a diplomatic reply, Beckman managed to avoid writing something she may have later regretted.

That's a good strategy. If the email you're contemplating writing is highly charged and emotional, some email experts advise delaying both the composition and sending for 24 hours, to let emotions settle.

"If you're experiencing strong emotions at the time of the email, don't send it at that time," says the American Academy of Etiquette's Lisa Taylor Richey. "If you're in a bad mood, in an emotional state of anger, walk away. Or if you're feeling emotion and the need to act on it, and you still need to make a statement, make it by phone call rather than email. The email can be permanent."

An even better approach, perhaps, is to compose the angry or emotional email in a word processing document, Beckman says. "Write it in Word, save it and close it, then take a break," she advises. "The longer the break, the better. Let it sit overnight."

"Shoot First, Think Later" an Ill-Conceived Strategy

It would require a criminal mastermind to be able to anticipate and avoid the myriad ways possible to mess up the perfect crime.

Similarly, there's almost no way to imagine all the ways to screw up when you're too quick with the "Send" button, says LitigationProofing's Eric M. Rosenberg.

Here are just a few of the landmines he's identified:

Failure to Note Automatic Recipient Address Completion. Many email systems can complete

an email recipient's address based on the first couple of characters typed into the box. But that automatic feature, designed to save a few strokes, is a frequent source of email misdelivery. "It's all too easy to assume the system has completed the correct name and correct address, without double checking," Rosenberg notes.

"Let's say a lawyer is writing to a colleague confidentially about a client with a name similar to the colleague's. The email system fills in the client's name and the confidential message never meant for the client's eyes is sent to that client ... Addressing an email without conscious thought and examination of the list of addresses before pressing 'Send' is like driving a car while talking on the cell phone. You risk making directional mistakes without any recollection of having done so."

Failure to Consider How Your Message Would Look in the Newspaper. Even when written for legitimate business purposes, many emails are loaded with content never intended for public consumption in a major newspaper, Rosenberg says.

Yet major newspapers are exactly where business email sometimes winds up being published.

Think Before You Email

For example, in an investigation of securities analysts conducted by New York State attorney general Eliot Spitzer, in which Spitzer contended the analysts were being insincere in their opinions, an email from a technology analyst became famous when Spitzer leaked it to newspapers. Sent from the analyst to another within the same firm, the email read as follows, Rosenberg says:

"This stock is a powder keg, given how aggressive we were on it earlier this year, and given the 'bad smell' comments that so many institutions are bringing up."

The same thought could have been written in a less controversial manner and never been worth the attention of a newspaper, Rosenberg comments. For example, the writer could have stated, "We are receiving some complaints from institutions unhappy with the stock's performance, after we had strongly recommended it. Please take care in what we write about this stock."

That statement would have been far less tantalizing to newspaper editors, reporters and readers, yet the same intent would have been clearly conveyed, Rosenberg says. Obviously, choice of words can be critical – and all the more reason to think before emailing.

Failure To Double Check Addresses on a Reply, Reply to All, cc, or bcc. If you are the recipient of a blind carbon copy (bcc) and decide to use the "reply to all" feature, you will disclose to all that you were a recipient of a copy of the original email, even though the sender intended for his or her own reasons not to disclose that fact, Rosenberg points out. "There's been a lot written about 'Reply to All,'" he says.

"It's just a landmine, because you may be saying something that you do not intend to go to every one of the recipients."

Richey is another observer who advises folks to be careful with the "Reply to All" feature. One of her friends, a partner at a Dallas law firm, had an assistant who keyed in a few disparaging, downright rude comments about a client in an email. The assistant unfortunately punched the "Reply to All" rather than "Reply" button.

"It was sent to everyone on the list, including the client about whom she had made the ugly remarks," Richey relates. "And she was fired."

It's worth noting email systems were originally created by people active in the technology arena, working in large groups and sharing information eagerly and widely, Rosenberg adds. The irony?

This broad sharing of information is just about 180 degrees removed from the way many corporate divisions that now rely on email systems need to work, he observes.

Mixing Personal Business with Real Business. Rosenberg recently compiled a "Seven Deadly Sins of Email" list, and crafting both personal and business email on company computers crowns the list. "When you're writing for a personal purpose, your content, speed of approach, and reflection are generally far different from when you're conveying a serious business message," he says. "People tend to use shorthand, exaggeration, humor, disputatious language and in general carry on in ways they might if they were talking to one another.

"My concern is that that email will be retained as if it's company email, and may be used in litigation, or in numerous other ways of embarrassment to the company."

Moreover, personal use of company email systems leads to what he terms "general email sloppiness." Using the company keyboard for personal use tends to decondition the emailer to the degree of caution he or she should be observing

when carefully wording business messages. As a result, instead of the corporate impacting the personal email, the informality and outright carelessness of the personal email slops over into the corporate email. "I only wish when people sat at the keyboard to type personal emails they used the same care we would hope they would use in typing corporate email," Rosenberg says. "But in fact, the reverse happens."

If you're tempted by the urge to cybernetically dispatch betting pools, chain letters or pornography on company time, be doubly wary of the "Send" button.

"There are any number of cases where personal exchanges that are disputatious or embarrassing for some other reason have inadvertently become public," Rosenberg notes, citing an incident that occurred several years ago involving a summer associate at a major New York City law firm. On his first week on the job, Rosenberg relates, the associate wrote the following email to a friend at another business: "Congrats on the CFA. I'm sure you're about to make v-p any day now. I'm busy doing jack shit."

The associate didn't think before sending. The message accidentally went out not just to the friend, but also to a list of other associates and partners at the firm, and then was forwarded to the media, presumably by one of the unintended recipients who found it amusing or otherwise remarkable.

It went on to appear in the *New Yorker* and the *New York Law Journal*, causing untold embarrassment not only to the associate, but to the firm.

Failure to Imagine the Possible Consequences of Your Email. Just how much hot water can a poorly conceived email get you into? Rosenberg suggests this hypothetical example:

Picture a college student close to a team in the NCAA Basketball Tournament. He learns something about a key player on the team and transmits that information in an email to the business email address of a friend who happens to be caught up in the throes of March Madness, and participating in a betting pool.

Then the team loses and, noting the odds began changing dramatically just before game time, the NCAA launches an investigation. The probe starts with an examination of emails in the university's server, focused on emails referenced by names of players. Imagine that leads back to

the student who wrote the first email, and from there to the server of the employer for whom the recipient of the first email works.

Though the twists and turns of this hypothetical scenario seem implausible, they really aren't, Rosenberg asserts. So the next time you're tempted to pound out and dispatch an email of any kind without separating those two actions with some thought, remember Rosenberg's words:

"Misdelivery, retention and investigation on the recipient's side, surveillance on your side, maybe surveillance at the recipient's firm: There really is no end to the ways in which what you think is a personal email might become a public email."

Chris - You were great in that presentation to the institutional investors this morning. You made ABC stock seem way better than the dog that it is. Suckers!

Ed

Can you envision "Suckers!" in a newspaper headline?

Chapter 6

Emails are Forever

There's an innate contradiction to email. What starts out as fleeting and ephemeral as a spring blossom or gentle summer breeze can end up as permanent as a granite monolith. "Email doesn't go away," says attorney and email expert Jeremy Mishkin. "And even when you attempt to make it go away, it doesn't go away."

Or, as LRN's Dov Seidman reports, if you miscommunicate in an email, "You have a paper trail, retrievable and searchable forever, or practically forever. Even though email can lull you into the bad habit of being quick, informal and less than complete, the fact it lasts forever should compel people to develop real skills in this mode of communication."

Built-In Durability

On most email systems, the email you send travels through more than one server, where it's retained for periods of time varying widely and depending heavily on the legal requirements and behaviors of the companies controlling the servers, says LitigationProofing's Eric M. Rosenberg. What you type can also end up on the hard drive of the machinery on which you're working. And if you're working on a transportable computer, it can end up on that device in a very permanent way.

Why, you ask, isn't it eliminated when you click, "Delete"? Because unlike erasing a tape recording, you're not erasing your email, Rosenberg explains. Instead, you're informing the computer

that the space is available to be overwritten.

You're not actually writing over the deleted email as you would record over a previously recorded song. What's more, you may not over-write it for some time. And when that email IS overwritten, perhaps only every tenth character will be affected.

"People who engage in the activity of finding out what's on the memory of the computer are forensic experts, and they can frequently recover items you thought you had erased, because the items had not been overwritten in full," he says. "You're absolutely not deleting anything. You're not deleting it from the machine you're working on, and you're certainly not deleting it from the places it has had to go in transit to the ultimate recipient. This is so whether the email is company email or personal email."

To Recover or Not?

Still, he notes, there is nothing predictable about the recoverability of any particular email. The chance of it being recovered will vary widely depending on the amount of financial and intel-lectual resources expended in an effort to unearth the message, Rosenberg says.

Emails are Forever

Imagine, if you will, that you have deleted an email from your home computer. The email has gone through an email account with, say, America Online, and from there to your friend, who has an email account with another Internet Service Provider. The email will be retained for a period of time at America Online and at the other ISP. It will also be retained in some manner on your friend's computer.

If it's simply a matter of you wishing you had that email back to read over again, it's not likely you would expend the time, effort and money to retrieve it.

But if a lawsuit hinged on the recovery of the email, ample resources would be available to try to recover it at each of its stops along the way, as well as at its ultimate destination, Rosenberg says.

Back to Bite You

And there's every good reason those resources would be expended, Mishkin observes. "Today, many attorneys are finding that email that either was sent by their client or to their client is becoming the most significant piece of evidence in a trial," he says. "That's because it looks like a doc-

ument written by or to their client. In normal conversation, people spout all kinds of garbage that is half-baked, non-baked or completely wrong, and there's no trace of it, so it doesn't come back to bite you.

"But email comes back to bite you. So instead of saying something dumb that no one ever hears, you're essentially dumb on prime time TV. No one physically typing a memo and signing it would ever put down on paper a small fraction of what they're willing to put into email. There's very little awareness that these messages are capable of coming back to haunt you months and years later."

Such hauntings can lead to embarrassments both professional and personal, according to Rosenberg. For instance, some professionals – whether due to hubris or simple brain cramps – succumb to inexplicable urges to write to friends about sensitive business matters that should never leave the confines of their office suite.

The most famous such case involved a securities analyst who penned an email to a friend detailing the real reason he had bestowed an improved opinion upon a major telecom stock. That email was recovered, and was used as evidence by the Securities and Exchange

Commission (SEC) in forcing the man out of the analyst profession.

"There's also some tendency for people to write personal email on company systems, because they want to avoid the email being seen by someone at home, who might have access to the family's personal email," Rosenberg adds. "For example, writing to an old or present paramour, and not wanting the email to be seen by the spouse. It never ceases to amaze me."

Saved, But For How Long?

Some businesses establish legal requirements that outgoing and incoming emails be saved for some period of time, Rosenberg reports. Examples include the community of broker dealers and investment advisors, where SEC rules require retention for periods ranging from three to five years.

("That's a lot of retention," Rosenberg notes.)

Retention of certain accounting records that could include email is also required under the mandates of the Sarbanes Oxley Act for periods of several years.

Many businesses end up retaining email for some period of time as a matter of protection

against business interruption. For example, if a natural disaster were to affect a firm's computer servers, from which email is transmitted and where it's typically stored, the company would want to ensure it would be able to return to business promptly following the catastrophe.

For that reason, many businesses create a tape backup of the contents of the server each evening after the close of business. Those backups are stored at sites physically removed from the business itself. Good practice would suggest those tapes shouldn't be retained any longer than necessary. For that reason, many companies set up a rotation in which older tapes are discarded and newer tapes retained in their place.

However, there is much variation from one company to the next in the way the rotation is handled, according to Rosenberg. In a major case tried in 2005, the failure by a defendant in a securities fraud action to produce all backup tapes when properly requested in discovery resulted in a ruling by the court preventing the defendant from being able to assert it had not made fraudulent representations.

It's also important to recognize that retention impacts not just email, but instant messaging as well, he adds. "The method by which that communication may be retained, and the length of time the system retains it, may be quite different in the case of instant messaging," he says.

"Instant messaging uses a different application, and certain types of instant messaging don't retain that string of back-and-forth communication. But an instant messaging communication is regarded in the same manner as an email communication in terms of rules and regulations pertaining to retention. However, the actual systems, and the manner in which it is captured, may be quite different than that of email."

Don't assume voicemail is immune from recovery either. According to Rosenberg, in some company voicemail systems, a message left as voicemail will turn up as an email attachment, and even that is retained.

All this having been said, one truth is very evident. It's best to assume that email you're sending can be recovered.

Says Rosenberg: "Unlike telephone conversations and old-fashioned business letters, what you type in the business or personal setting in electronic communications should be regarded as permanent – and searchable."

Chapter 7

Legal Implications of Email

Email written or handled the wrong way can result in you or your company encountering needless legal liability. Examples of this phenomenon abound, but for brevity's sake, here are but three ways this can happen:

Giving In To Your Baser Instincts

According to LitigationProofing's Eric M. Rosenberg, a category of email particularly damaging in a court of law involves exaggerations, gallows humor, temper tantrums, boasts, guarantees, rumor mongering, the leaking of sensitive information and/or the spreading of rumors. "It's a series of behaviors that in one way or another is excessive," he says. "Any content that's not true fact can be posed as supposed fact in litigation, leaving the writer with the difficult task of explaining why excessive language was included only for attention-getting effect."

An especially insidious sub-species of this breed of email involves what Rosenberg calls "corporate humor." Not unlike gallows humor, it surfaces when people face difficult business problems, and resort to humor to defuse the tension they're experiencing. "It comes to look particularly bad because it appears to be making light of a serious problem," he says.

A memorable example occurred during legal proceedings involving a pharmaceutical company marketing the diet drug Phen-Phen.

In what appeared to be frustration with his assigned task with the company, an employee

wrote an email that later became known in court proceedings. In the email, the employee asked a colleague, "Do I have to look forward to spending my waning years writing checks to fat people worried about a silly lung problem?"

Perhaps more than any other excessive expression, gallows humor hurts in litigation. "Probably because it can be perceived to show some acknowledgement of guilt, and appears to be uncaring about the consequences of that guilt," Rosenberg says. "There's some anecdotal evidence juries believe the same thought in email more than if it were in some other, more formal, corporate document. The reason? They believe the email is a more frank and candid expression of the writer's feelings."

A Call To Action

Another type of email situation fraught with peril from a legal standpoint involves email that requires corrective action.

Though we all receive more email than we want and are hard-pressed to wade through all of it, we can be presumed to have knowledge of the contents of an email that we may or may not have read, if it arrived on our workstation, Rosenberg points out. "Certainly once you have opened an email, you will be found to be knowledgeable as to its contents," he notes.

"Particularly if it relates to an area of your responsibility. Therefore it is important to give proper attention, often through counsel to your firm, with respect to received emails that raise problems. The principles of problem elevation under the terms of the Sarbanes Oxley Act apply to information received through email."

That means that if an incident involving misbehavior, for instance financial misreporting, is brought to your attention in a business setting, you must in turn bring that information to the attention of management so it can be dealt with by your employer. "If you become aware of misbehavior, you must elevate it," Rosenberg says. "In other words, take it to a higher level within the company."

Heeding Copyright Laws

Failing to heed copyright laws can also result in court appearances. The act of forwarding electronic clippings in an email implies the possible violation of copyright laws, Rosenberg says. However, the issue is very circumstance specific.

If you are working for a business that prizes intellectual property – for instance a company in the recording industry – it would likely seem particularly inconsistent with those corporate priorities to apparently violate copyright laws by forwarding electronic newspaper clippings. "It would look particularly hypocritical in an industry dependent upon the creating and protection of intellectual property," Rosenberg argues.

Some of the most egregious examples of email misuse remain confidential from public review, as they often result in case settlements not made public, Rosenberg concludes. But given the fact that email is routinely required to be exchanged in civil and criminal litigation discovery, the examples of exacerbation of litigation liability through thoughtless email are growing.

Legal Implications of Email

```
000                    Compose: bike lawsuit                      ⊖
 📷         📇          ABC        📎 ▾      🔒 ▾      📥 ▾         ✂
Send      Contacts     Spell      Attach    Security    Save

From:  ED AVIS <edavis@marionstreetpress.com>  - edavis@marionstreetpress.com  ▲▼

  ▾      To:  📇  jane@dietbike.com




Subject:  bike lawsuit
```

hi jane - yeah, i heard about that lawsuit, too. like we were supposed
to know the weight limits on those bikes? i mean, if you're THAT fat, go
on a diet before you get on the exercise bike!

ed

The plaintiff's lawyer will be SO happy to find this email on your server.

Chapter 8

Toward More Civil Emailing

In this final chapter, we ask a simple question: Is it possible to bring to the exciting, dynamic, cutting edge technology of email the kind of consideration and civility many identify with a bygone age?

For the answer, we turn to no less an authority

than P.M. Forni, professor of Romance Languages at Baltimore's Johns Hopkins University, and author of *Choosing Civility: The Twenty-Five Rules of Considerate Conduct* (St. Martin's Press, 2002).

Dressing Down Communication

What we see each business day in email, Forni says, is a reflection of the utter informality that characterizes our everyday life. Not only are we becoming more and more informal as a society, but information technology is actually accelerating that process. "When it comes to using technology," he says. "It seems like it's dress-down Friday all the time."

Two factors carry the potential to create uncivil email communication, he says:

We live in a society of total disclosure. Informality rules the day, and in this age of total disclosure, it's easy to forego restraint in communication. It sometimes seems anything can be said of anybody to everybody. In other words, it's easy to say things we come to regret.

Email is a form of long-distance, not in-presence, communication. Email stands in bold contrast to face-to-face communication and telephone communication, where the other person is

present. When people are physically present, or present on the phone, we are more watchful and in general more careful to avoid breaking the rules of accepted niceties. But, Forni says, when we use email, the other person is not present, and we're therefore less likely to exercise restraint. "This is a real problem," he says.

It's a problem because, as we've learned, there is no such thing as a private email. So if we write something we come to regret, we have to live with it for the foreseeable future. "It's troubling and perplexing that many leaders in companies have not really internalized the very elementary notion that there really isn't such a thing as a private email," Forni observes. "Employers have the right to look at their employees' emails, which are routinely recorded and stored, and hackers can access computer in-boxes. It's only slightly more private than skywriting."

Breaking etiquette rules in email is also a problem because emailing is not in any sense a traditional communication form. Thus, we've become accustomed to using this new technology in ways that make us believe the traditional boundaries of communication are now obsolete. Since email is a revolutionary and innovative technology of communication, we use it as though we can forego the traditional rules of deference, respect and discretion, Forni argues.

As a result, emailers all too often hurt the feelings of people at the receiving end of their cybernetic messages. They mar their professional reputations. They stain the images of their employers.

And they conduct themselves in ways decidedly not in the best interests of business. The result is an injection of negativity into the ordinary course of doing business, Forni says. "It affects, in a negative way, the quality of life for all concerned."

Corrective Actions

The chronic and widespread misuse of email needn't become a universal and permanent phenomenon, however. Forni suggests several strategies to turn a medium that often takes unpleasant twists and turns into one that works toward positive good:

Adopt A Mindset. Everyone who uses email should strive for a heightened consciousness about what this technology is, what it does, and what the consequences of using it mindlessly can

be, Forni says.

Just remembering that there is no such thing as a private email, and that emails are indeed forever, can be a good beginning toward adopting this mindset. "In the past, you could get away with an intemperate outburst in person, or even over the phone," he says. "Today, if you indulge in such behavior online, the technology may not be so forgiving. So awareness and sensitivity and professionalism are what we need in order to approach, at our best, this great means of communication, and make it work for us."

The Positive Side of Email. When does email get sent? All too often, when we need something from others, or when we feel the urge to vent our feelings. It's just as important, however, that we use email to show appreciation, to say thank you, to offer support, to express concern.

"It would be good to think of email as something to use not only when we need to, but when others need to hear from us in a positive fashion," Forni says.

Avoid the Slop. Approach email as a means of demonstrating your professionalism. Be careful with spelling, grammar and punctuation.

"There is no excuse for not doing that," Forni says. "No sterling professional will fire off sloppy messages. The emails you send say something about who you are, and reflect on your company or organization."

Don't Write and Click. Rather than keyboarding and then sending in one unbroken, fluid motion, take some time between those two acts.

Write. Then read. Read once for form, and once for content, Forni advises. And if you realize the message is one you would be embarrassed to communicate in person, reconsider whether you should send the email at all.

Don't Act on Impulse. If you're uncertain about the tone or content of the message, set it aside for 15 minutes, and then make your decision upon re-reading the email. Impulse can be dangerous in any walk of life. But acting on impulse is doubly dangerous in the cybernetic world, because the technology can turn that momentary impulse into a lasting testament to the sender's impetuousness, he adds.

The Latins of antiquity anticipated the prob-

lems that one day would surface with the coming of email, Forni says. They had a saying that not only was true in their time, but foreshadowed the age when quickly and easily dashed-off missives would wing their way from sender to recipient instantly, and would be documented, recorded and stored for posterity. The Latins' saying, roughly translated, was:

"Once you have uttered a word, it cannot be unuttered."

In this age of email, Forni notes, that's never been more true.

Toward More Civil Emailing

Sample Company Email Policy

Companies large and small may want to incorporate the following twelve points regarding proper email etiquette and protocol when crafting a company email policy.

1. Company emails should always feature the respectful salutations, appropriate courtesy and thorough professionalism of a business letter.

2. Company emails should be kept brief, concise and to the point.

3. Company emails should be proofread once for content and once for style.

4. Company emails should be carefully addressed to the proper recipient.

5. Company emails should focus on business, not personal, matters.

6. Company emails should be written with the understanding they may be reviewed.

Sample Company Email Policy

7. Company emails should be written with the expectation they will be stored.

8. Company emails should be written with the knowledge they are not anonymous.

9. Company emails should be written with the knowledge they may be used in a court of law.

10. Company emails should not be used for emotional or angry messages.

11. Company emails are the only emails that should be written on company time.

12. Company emails reflect on the company as well as the writer.

How To Contact Sources
Contributing To This Book:

Wendy Hart Beckman, author of *Communication Tools Made Easy*
beckcomm@fuse.net

Cheryl Dellasega, GNP, professor of humanities
Penn State College of Medicine, Hershey, Pa.
Author of *Mean Girls Grown Up*
cdellasega@psu.edu
www.cheryldellasega.com

Ted Demopoulus, consultant and speaker
Demopoulus Associates, Durham, NH
603-231-8782
ted@demop.com

Charlotte Ford, author of *21st Century Etiquette: Charlotte Ford's Guide to Manners for the Modern Age*

P.M. Forni, author of *Choosing Civility; The Twenty-Five Rules of Considerate Conduct*
Department of Romance Languages and Literatures
Johns Hopkins University, Baltimore
410-516-8047
forni@jhu.edu
www.jhu.edu/civility

Contact Information

Randy Hines, APR, associate professor of public relations and advertising
Susquehanna University, Selinsgrove, PA
Author of *The Writer's Toolbox: A Comprehensive Guide for PR and Business Communication*
hines@susqu.edu

Jeremy Mishkin, partner
Montgomery, McCracken, Walker & Rhoads, Philadelphia
215-772-7246
jmishkin@mmwr.com
www.mmwr.com

Lisa Taylor Richey, president
The American Academy of Etiquette, Philadelphia
800-839-4640
www.americanetiquette.com

Eric M. Rosenberg, president
Litigation Proofing LLC, Mamaroneck, NY
914-777-7321
www.litigationproofing.com

Dov Seidman, CEO
LRN, Los Angeles
800-529-6366
www.LRN.com
info@LRN.com

Index

Index

Index